THE STORY OF SPACE
PROBES TO THE
PLANETS

Steve Parker

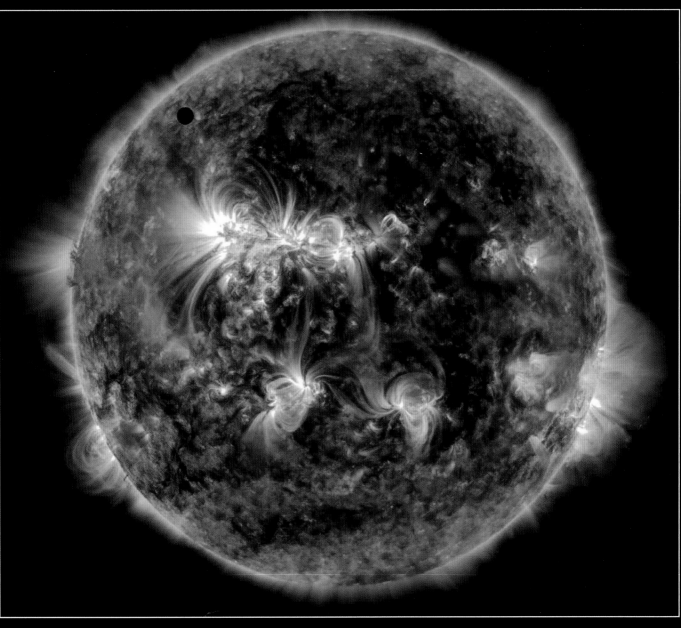

A⁺

Smart Apple Media

Published by Smart Apple Media, an imprint of Black Rabbit Books
P.O. Box 3263, Mankato, Minnesota 56002
www.blackrabbitbooks.com

Produced by David West ⚇ Children's Books
6 Princeton Court, 55 Felsham Road, London SW15 1AZ

Designed by Gary Jeffrey

Library of Congress Cataloging-in-Publication Data

Cataloging-in-Publication Data is available from the Library of Congress.
ISBN 978-1-62588-077-2

CSPIA compliance information: DWCB14FCP
011014

9 8 7 6 5 4 3 2 1

All images courtesy of NASA except: p6tr, NASA/Max Planck, p6b, NASA Goddard Photo and Video; p7tr, NASA/Johns Hopkins University Applied Physics Laboratory, p7bl, NorJerry MagnuM Porsbjer; p8b, ESA - AOES Medialab; p10bl, ESA/MPS/DLR/IDA; p11m, p17br, p23bl, p27m, NASA/JPL; p12bl, NASA/USGS; p13tr, Jim Bell (Cornell University), Mike Wolff (Space Science Institute), and NASA; p15t, NASA/JPL (Corby Waste), p15mr, NASA-JPL-Cornell, p15ml, NASA/JPL; modified/coloured by D Mitriy, p15b, NASA/JPL-Caltech/USGS/Cornell University; p16l, NASA-JPL-Caltech-Malin Space Science Systems; p17ml. NASA - JPL-Caltech - Olivier de Goursac, p17m, b, NASA/JPL-Caltech/MSSS; p21tr, p24bl, NASA/JPL/Space Science Institute, p21r, SA/JPL/Space Science Institute; p22t, The Hubble Heritage Team (AURA/STScI/NASA); p24mr, NASA/JPL-Caltech/Space Science Institute; p25tr, NASA/JPL/University of Arizona, p25b, NASA/JPL-Caltech; p26t, NASA/Johns Hopkins Applied Physics Laboratory, p26l, NASA/JPL-Caltech/UCLA/MPS/DLR/IDA/PSI, p26br, Rick Sternbach/KISS, p26r, NASA/JPL/JHUAPL, p26bl, NASA, ESA, and A. Feild (STScI); p27 tl, Halley Multicolor Camera Team, Giotto Project, ESA, p27tr, br, ESA; p28tl, H. Weaver (JHU/APL), A. Stern (SwRI), and the HST Pluto Companion Search Team, p28t, Lunar and Planetary Institute, p28l, NASA/Johns Hopkins University Applied Physics Laboratory/Southwest Research Institute, p28r, C m handler; p29r, b, ESO-L. Calçada

CONTENTS

Space probe Cassini has been in orbit around Saturn since 2004, making hundreds of flybys of the giant planet and its dozens of moons.

INTRODUCTION

The Solar System is vast—4.6 trillion miles from the Sun to the outer reaches. Its eight planets, with their moons, are tiny specks spread far apart in the great emptiness. Our exploration of space, which began over 50 years ago, has mainly focused on these planets and moons.

We have overcome such gigantic distances by using unmanned probes. They are programmed to fly close to planets and even land on them, gather data, record images, and transmit the information back to Earth. Knowledge of other planets is vital. It helps us to understand how our own planet came to be, how it is changing now, and what might be waiting in the future.

Mobile probes like NASA's Mars explorer Curiosity are called rovers. Partly remote-controlled and partly robotic, they can explore a distant and hostile environment without the risk and expense of human spaceflight.

SOLAR PROBES

Categorized a "yellow dwarf," our Sun is a medium-size star halfway through its 10-billion-year lifecycle. This huge body makes up almost 99 percent of the total mass the Solar System that spins around it.

INSIDE THE SUN

. **CORE** Thermonuclear reactor
. **RADIATIVE ZONE** Heat spreads outward
. **CONVECTION ZONE** Columns of heat rise and fall
. **PHOTOSPHERE** Visible surface of the atmosphere
. **CHROMOSPHERE** Thin layer of wispy hydrogen
. **CORONA** Wide area of hot plasma radiating outward

EMPIRE OF THE SUN

Like all stars, the Sun began as a vast, intensely cold cloud of dust and hydrogen atoms. This collapsed inward under its own gravity, clumped together, and ignited. The Sun is made of 74 percent hydrogen, 24 percent helium, and 2 percent heavy elements. Its core pressure, and temperature of 23 million °F (13 million °C), are high enough to rip apart hydrogen atoms and reform them as helium—a process called nuclear fusion. The incredible energy radiates in columns to blaze on the photosphere as light and heat.

NASA's SDO (Solar Dyna probing the Sun's m various rays 2010

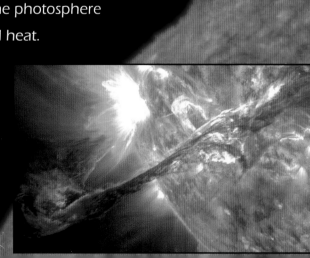

The Sun's charged particles meet Earth's magnetic field and cause polar lights or auroras (above). Plasma eruptions from its surface (right) can cause magnetic storms on Earth.

The **SUN** is mainly **PLASMA—neither** a **gas**, **liquid**, nor **solid**, but more like **PURE ENERGY**.

SOLAR PROBE PLUS

1. **THERMAL SHIELD** Carbon composites
2. **PRIMARY SOLAR ARRAYS** For use early in the mission and then stowed behind the heat shield
3. **COMMUNICATIONS ANTENNA**
4. **SECONDARY SOLAR ARRAY** Liquid cooled, deployed on final approach to the Sun's surface

Solar Probe Plus will speed around the Sun three times faster than the Helios craft.

PROBING THE INFERNO

Probes have analyzed the interior of the Sun, and on its surface observed sunspots—magnetic storms larger than Earth. The surface of the Sun is 10,300 °F (5,700 °C), "cool" enough to be approached by robot spacecraft. In 2018 Solar Probe Plus will become the most intrepid solar explorer yet. To study the outer corona up close, its instruments are protected by the shadow of a special carbon heat shield.

Since 1995 NASA's Solar and Heliospheric Observatory, SOHO, has been sending real-time data on space weather—variations in the solar wind from the Sun.

The Sun throws out a huge arc of energy, or "prominence," big enough to engulf all the planets. Surprisingly the Sun's visible surface, the photosphere, is hundreds of times cooler than the invisible corona that surrounds it.

The **SUN**'s energy **particles** spend an **average** of **200,000 YEARS** traveling around **inside** their **star**, then after **RELEASE** they reach **Earth** in just **EIGHT MINUTES**.

MERCURY

1. **CRUST** Up to 200 miles (320 km) thick
2. **MANTLE** Chiefly silicate rocky minerals
3. **CORE** Mainly liquid iron

Battered, scorched Mercury is the smallest planet in the Solar System. Closest to the Sun, its atmosphere boiled away long ago. This super-hot world is one of the most difficult, hazardous places a probe might visit.

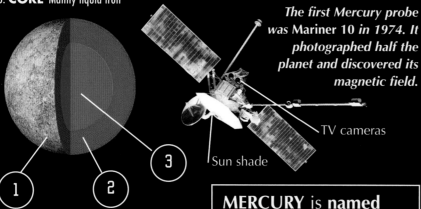

The first Mercury probe was Mariner 10 in 1974. It photographed half the planet and discovered its magnetic field.

TV cameras

Sun shade

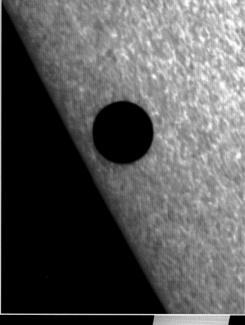

1

2

3

BLASTED WORLD

The Sun shines on Mercury 10 times more strongly than on Earth. The difference between

> **MERCURY** is **named** after the **Ancient** Roman **MESSENGER** to the **GODS.** Its **year** (one Sun orbit) is **88** Earth **days.**

night and day temperatures is greatest in the Solar System, from -343 °F (-173 °C)—which would liquefy oxygen—to 790 °F (421 °C) that could melt lead. Mercury also rotates slowly, so one Mercurian day lasts 58 Earth days. Its large metal core makes it the second densest planet after Earth. However Mercury's small size means, unlike other planets, it could not hang onto any of its ancient atmosphere.

So close to the Sun, Mercury is hard to observe from Earth. It is mostly seen in transit, or passing in front of, our blazing star.

MMO Orbiter

Sun shield

Mercury Transfer Module

MPO Orbiter

Ion engines

The joint ESA (European Space Agency) and JAXA (Japan Space Agency) probe BepiColombo should arrive on Mercury in 2022. On it, JAXA's Mercury Magnetospheric Orbiter (MMO) will analyze the planet's magnetic field while ESA's Mercury Planet Orbiter (MPO) maps the planet in greater detail than ever before.

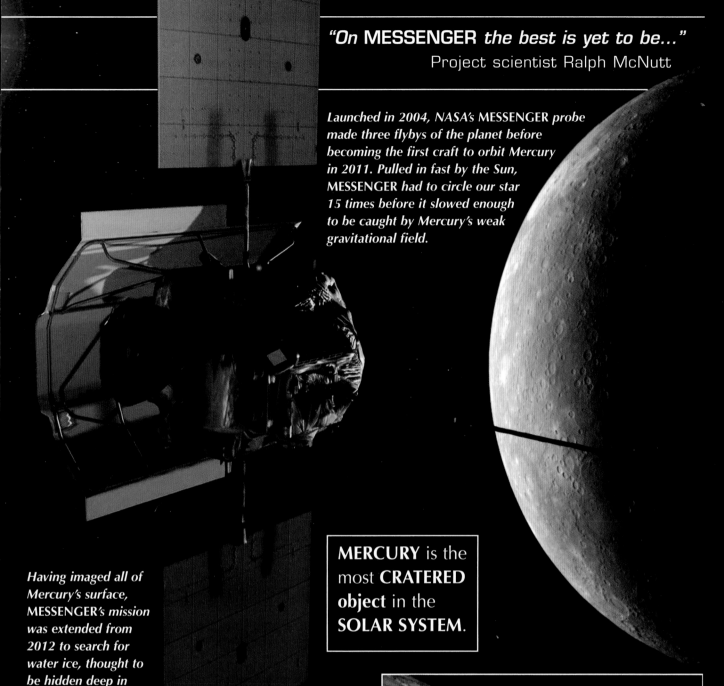

Launched in 2004, NASA's MESSENGER probe made three flybys of the planet before becoming the first craft to orbit Mercury in 2011. Pulled in fast by the Sun, MESSENGER had to circle our star 15 times before it slowed enough to be caught by Mercury's weak gravitational field.

Having imaged all of Mercury's surface, MESSENGER's mission was extended from 2012 to search for water ice, thought to be hidden deep in polar craters.

MERCURY is the most **CRATERED object** in the **SOLAR SYSTEM**.

A MILLION HITS

Without an atmosphere to protect it, Mercury has borne the full impact of every space object attracted onto its surface by the nearby Sun. Some were so big, they buckled the planet on the far side of their strike site. As well as documenting these scars, *MESSENGER* also discovered many volcanoes. Mercury holds vital clues to the origin of our Solar System's inner, rocky worlds.

MESSENGER photographed Mercury's Caloris Basin in great detail. Caloris (here in yellow) is one of the largest impact craters in the entire Solar System. The orange splotches, lower left, show volcanic vents.

VENUS

Sometimes called "Earth's evil twin," Venus hides its surface beneath thick clouds of sulfur fumes. It is also the hottest planet in the Solar System—too scorching for any form of life.

INSIDE VENUS

1. **ATMOSPHERE** 96% carbon dioxide, 3.5% nitrogen, particles of sulfur dioxide, droplets of sulfuric acid
2. **ROCKY CRUST** 90% resurfaced by molten lava
3. **MANTLE** Similar depth to Earth, 1,700 miles (2,700 km)
4. **CORE** Probably part-liquid and part-solid, possibly metallic

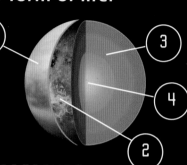

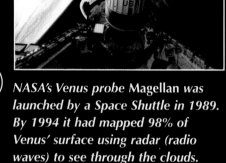

NASA's Venus *probe* Magellan *was launched by a Space Shuttle in 1989. By 1994 it had mapped 98% of Venus' surface using radar (radio waves) to see through the clouds.*

ESA's Venus Express *orbiter (below) reached the planet in 2006. Its long-term mission was to study Venus' atmosphere. The craft imaged cloud formations (inset), confirmed the presence of lightning and found evidence of recent volcano activity.*

UNDER PRESSURE

Venus is a similar size to Earth and has a similar mass and gravity, but crucially it lies closer to the Sun and has almost no magnetic field. For the first billion or so years of its life, Venus probably had oceans, but solar radiation gradually boiled the hydrogen and oxygen into space, leaving vast amounts of carbon dioxide. Fueled by global volcanic activity, Venus became hostage to a runaway "greenhouse effect" that sends surface temperatures soaring to 880 °F (460 °C). Its surface pressure is 92 times Earth's—equivalent to being 3,000 ft (910 meters) under our ocean.

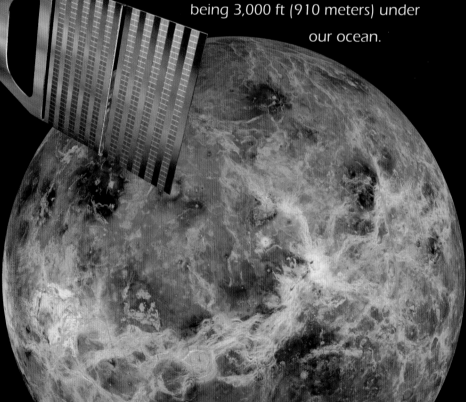

A composite radar map by Magellan *shows Venus' "young" surface—less than 500 million years old, and 90% volcanic rock.*

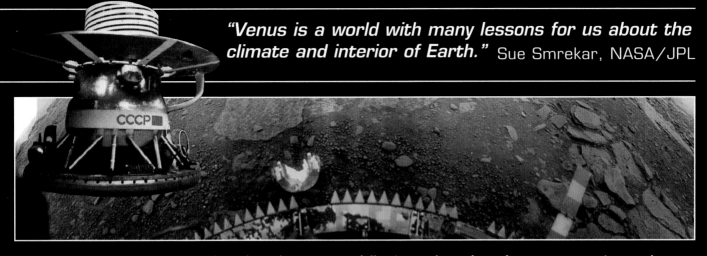

The only probes to successfully picture the surface of Venus were Russia's tough Venera landers. Venera 13 (inset) sent this eerie panoramic view of its surroundings.

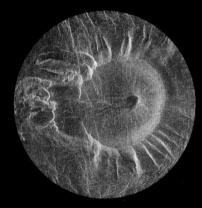

Venus is pockmarked by 1,600 volcanoes. The "tick" type, named because it resembles a bug, is unique to the planet.

"HELLISH" SURFACE

Venus is a supremely hostile environment for probes. *Venera 13's* camera windows were made of thick quartz, its instruments encased in a pressure hull, and the whole lander was designed to last only 30 minutes while it sent data to its orbiting partner craft. As well as imaging, *Venera* analyzed a sample of Venusian dirt before imploding in a fiery heap 127 minutes after touchdown. Venus rotates the opposite way to the other planets. It also appears to have a single tectonic plate in its crust, as opposed to Earth's many plates. To solve such mysteries, more probes will go to this shrouded world.

VENUS spins **more SLOWLY** than any other **planet**. Each **VENUSIAN DAY** lasts **243 Earth** days.

NASA plans an aerial Venus probe with metal bellows to resist the crushing pressure. It will look for evidence to show how and when Venus' climate became overwhelmed by carbon dioxide.

An artist's impression shows what it might be like to stand on the surface of Venus. As hurricane-force winds scour the surface, lightning arcs down from sulfuric acid clouds, whose droplets vaporize the instant they fall.

MARS – VIKING

Fourth and last of the inner, rocky planets, Mars was the second alien world probed by landers. A global desert, Mars is a half-sized, freeze-dried version of Earth.

In 1971 Mariner 9 was the first space probe to orbit Mars. For months a planet-wide duststorm blocked the view. When it cleared Mariner 9 was able to map almost the entire planet.

INSIDE MARS

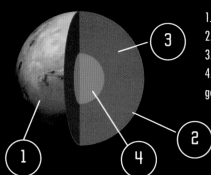

1. **ATMOSPHERE** 96% carbon dioxide, 1.9% nitrogen, argon
2. **CRUST** Average 30 miles (50 km) thick
3. **MANTLE** Silicate mineral rocks, similar to Earth's
4. **CORE** Iron and other sulphides, relatively inactive, generates only a weak magnetic field

Mariner 9 found Mons Olympus, the tallest peak in the Solar System. At 15 miles (25 km) it is three times higher than Everest.

Our **GRAND CANYON** could **fit** into a **SIDE BRANCH** of **Mars'** great **VALLE MARINARIS.**

Composite view of Mars, including Valle Marinaris, imaged by the Viking *orbiter.*

SCULPTED WORLD

The 1971–72 success of *Mariner 9* spurred NASA to build two combined orbiter/landers for Mars. *Viking 1* reached Mars orbit in June 1976, with *Viking 2* two months later.

A mock-up Viking *lander with famous US space expert and cosmologist Carl Sagan.*

The orbiters scanned Mars for landing sites and prepared to act as data relays for their landers. Their searches revealed a world with geological features similar to Earth's—some only explained by torrents of flowing water. Excitement ran high as the two *Viking* landers were released and de-orbited to begin their descent.

Mars' atmosphere is so thin, equivalent to 22 miles (35 km) altitude on Earth. that it offers little resistance to landers slowing for touchdown.

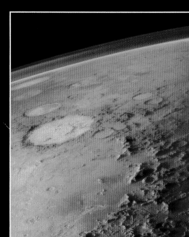

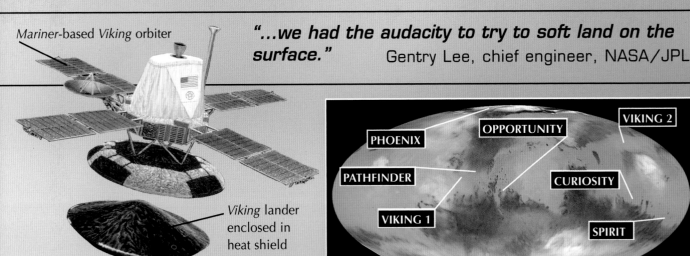

Mariner-based *Viking* orbiter

Viking lander enclosed in heat shield

PHOENIX

OPPORTUNITY

VIKING 2

PATHFINDER

CURIOSITY

VIKING 1

SPIRIT

Viking landers were sterilized to prevent Mars being contaminated with Earth germs. They used a complex sequence of heat shields, parachutes, and landing rockets to arrive safely on the surface.

The **Viking** *landers continued to send data for six years. Their success paved the way for many future Martian landers and exploration rovers, as shown above.*

LIFE ON MARS?

The *Viking* landings were NASA's biggest triumph since the *Apollo* moonshots. As well as imaging, the landers profiled the atmosphere and surface, taking soil samples for analysis in their high-tech biological mini-laboratories. Some experts believe the results showed evidence of life, but this remains controversial. Because *Viking* was so colossally expensive, following missions had different priorities.

Viking 1 *scooped soil samples from Chryse Planitia, an ancient crater in the Martian lowlands.*

Viking 2 *landed in Utopia Planitia, an area strewn with similar-sized rocks and thought to be once a seabed.*

VIKING cost **US $1 BILLION** in **1976** dollars—**US $4 BILLION today**, almost **DOUBLE** the **cost** of **MARS SCIENCE LAB.**

MARS – MERs

In 1997, NASA sent the first of three robotic Mars Exploration Rovers (MERs) to the red planet, heralding an exciting new era in Solar System exploration.

Mars' **ORBIT** is **OFF-CENTER compared** to **EARTH'S** orbit. Each **MARTIAN year** lasts **TWO Earth YEARS**.

NASA's Mars missions pioneered a new airbag-cushioned landing method.

Mars Pathfinder's lander (later renamed Sagan) touched down in 1997. It carried a miniature rover, Sojourner.

MOBILE GEOLOGISTS

The success of technologies in 1997's *Mars Pathfinder* led to two bigger MERs, Mars Exploration Rovers, *Spirit* and *Opportunity*. They arrived on the Red Planet in 2004. Their main mission was to search the Martian terrain for evidence of past water activity and thereby discover whether the Mars environment was ever favorable to life. The MERs' mission time was set at 90 days and they were not expected to travel more than 2,000 feet (600 meters) from their landing sites.

MER SYSTEMS

1. **PANORAMIC CAMERAS**
2. **NAVIGATION CAMERAS**
3. **SOLAR ARRAYS**
4. **ROBOT ARM**
5. **MOBILITY SYSTEM** Six one-wheel rocker/bogies, wheels treaded with cleats for grip
6. **BODY** Protects rover battery and electronics, heated by miniature radioisotope generator
7. **ANTENNA** Directional
8. **ANTENNA** Wide beam

MER's average speed is 0.4 inches (10 mm) per second, halting every 10 seconds to spend 20 seconds analyzing the terrain.

Microscope camera

Robot arm features an abrasion tool—the rover's version of a geologist's rock hammer and drill.

Rock abrasion tool

Spectrometer

Each wheel has its own motor, with the front and rear pairs steerable. The suspension system allows each wheel to climb over rocks twice its height yet keep all six wheels on the ground.

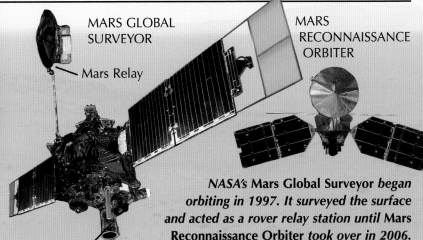

MARS GLOBAL SURVEYOR

Mars Relay

MARS RECONNAISSANCE ORBITER

Orbiter camera

Far above the rovers, up to four orbiters have been imaging and analyzing Mars in ever greater detail. These amazing swirls are Martian dry-ice caps at the north pole.

NASA's Mars Global Surveyor began orbiting in 1997. It surveyed the surface and acted as a rover relay station until Mars Reconnaissance Orbiter took over in 2006.

BEYOND EXPECTATION

Despite the wide-ranging Martian temperatures, from daytime highs of 95 °F (35 °C) to night lows of –225 °F (–143 °C), the MERs performed beautifully. During more than five mission extensions, *Spirit* discovered evidence of ancient hot springs, while *Opportunity* fought to free itself from a sand dune.

The MER's heat shield cases opened out flat like petals to allow them to exit in any direction.

Crucially, the rovers found twisted rocks and smooth pebbles eroded by water, showing Mars was once even wetter than scientists predicted. After six years and 4.8 miles (7.7 km) of travel, *Spirit* became hopelessly mired in soft sand and ended its mission. *Opportunity* was still roving over 10 years after its arrival.

In 2010 Opportunity *pictured this Martian "dust devil" mini-tornado.*

Spirit *photographed its own dust-covered solar panels. Periodic "cleaning events"— weather—scoured the panels bright again.*

Opportunity *has captured hundreds of detailed Martian panoramic landscapes, like this ancient crater eroded by wind.*

MARS – CURIOSITY

The latest robot to explore Mars is *Curiosity*, the rover of NASA's *Mars Science Lab*. Its mission is to discover whether Mars has, or has ever had, the means to sustain any form of life.

①
②
Ultra-high frequency antenna
③
⑦
High-gain antenna
Weather sensor
④
⑥

Curiosity's massive tool arm undergoes a systems test at NASA. The rover weighs 2,204 pounds (1 t).

Curiosity took this self-portrait at Gale Crater using the Mars Hand Lens Imager on its tool arm, which has a length of 7 feet (2 m).

⑤

Arm joint

CURIOSITY SYSTEMS

1. **CHEMCAM** Shoots a laser to analyze rock debris
2. **NAVCAMS** Black and white, two each side
3. **TWIN MASTCAMS** High- and medium-resolution color, still, video, different filters
4. **SAM** Rock analysis, looking for carbon and other elements essential for life (as we know it)
5. **CHEMIN** Measures levels of all Mars elements
6. **DAN** Radiation detector for subsurface water and ice
7. **BATTERY** Lithium, powered by Multi-Mission Radioisotope Thermoelectric Generator (MMRTG)
8. **MOBILITY** Six one-wheel rocker-bogies, independent drive and suspension, wheels studded with chevron cleats for grip

SPECIAL DELIVERY

On August 5, 2012, the *Mars Science Lab* capsule sped like a flaming bullet into the Martian atmosphere carrying NASA's latest planet probe. Delivering *Curiosity*, which was the weight of a small SUV, would be a $2.5 billion gamble. Fortunately, all went well and the most fully equipped and mobile rover yet—top speed of 295 feet (90 m) per hour!—began its mission.

⑧

Curiosity's landing site was in the fold of Gale Crater, 100 miles (160 km) wide and formed over 3.5 billion years ago. The crater is rich in minerals and ancient channels, indicating there was once flowing water.

"This mission is a critical planetary science mission..." NASA administrator Charles Bolden

After descending by parachute, the capsule heat shield popped off and a rocket-powered "skycrane" lowered the Curiosity rover down gently on a nylon cord cradle. After several failed Mars missions, the successful soft landing was a major triumph for NASA.

LAB GOES MOBILE

Curiosity is a mobile geology and chemistry lab whose primary mission is to look for carbon—the main chemical element that forms the microscopic building-blocks of life. The rover collected, grinded, and analyzed about 70 samples of soil and rock around Gale Crater. Other work included studying the Martian atmosphere and radiation levels, in case of future human exploration.

The rover travels 3–12 miles (4.8–19.3 km) per day. Based on its early performance, and those of previous rovers, in 2013 *Curiosity*'s mission was extended for several more years—at least.

The rotating tool head on Curiosity's arm is like a geologist's field kit for rapid, on-the-spot rock analysis.

Drill

Alpha Particle X-Ray Spectrometer (APXS)

Mars Hand Lens Imager (MAHLI)

Dust-Removal Tool

A telltale line of dots shows where CHEMCAM's laser fired into the dust next to a drilling site.

Future Mars missions might include bringing samples back to Earth, imagined here with a probe based on the 2005 Phoenix lander.

If its nuclear GENERATOR holds out, CURIOSITY could ROAM around MARS for 14 YEARS.

JUPITER

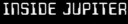

Relative size of Earth to Jupiter

Jupiter and its many moons resembles a solar system in miniature. Shrouded in powerful radiation fields, this giant is effectively a "nearly" star that was never big enough to ignite.

Veteran space probe Pioneer 10 was the first to visit Jupiter in 1973, learning about the powerful magnetosphere and strange liquid atmosphere of the so-called gas giant.

INSIDE JUPITER

1. **AMMONIA CLOUDS**
2. **FLUID HYDROGEN AND HELIUM**
3. **FLUID METALLIC HYDROGEN AND HELIUM** Similar in consistency to the liquid metal mercury
4. **PLANET CORE** Possibly made of iron or rock, or even liquid

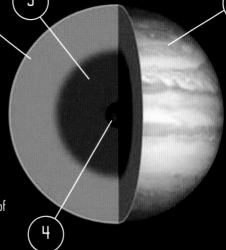

BY JOVE

Jupiter is the next planet after Mars, and beyond the Asteroid Belt, at its closest 390 million miles (628 million km) from Earth. NASA's *Pioneer 10* and *11* probes were the first to flyby and photograph, in 1973–74. Then in 1979 Jupiter was visited by NASA's *Voyager 1* and *2* as they headed for the outer Solar System. These missions discovered extra moons and the faint Jovian ring system, and filmed the planet's distinctively banded, swirling cloud movements.

JUPITER spins so **FAST, 28,300 mph** (45,300 km/h), **that it has a huge BULGE** in the **MIDDLE.**

BENEATH THE SURFACE

In 1989 NASA's *Galileo* probe launched from a US Space Shuttle. Its mission was to orbit the Jupiter system, send an entry probe down into the planet's atmosphere, and survey the largest Jovian moons. The results showed that Jupiter contained helium in similar proportions to the Sun and had intense radiation particles above its visible clouds. *Galileo* also sent pictures of Comet Shoemaker-Levy 9 being swallowed up by the gas giant.

Its main antenna furled shut, Galileo waits to be fitted with upper stage booster rockets at Kennedy Space Center, 1989.

This image, clearly showing Jupiter's Great Red Spot, was taken by the Hubble Space Telescope. Earth would fit comfortably inside the huge spot—a storm that is known to have raged for over 300 years.

MASSIVE JUPITER acts like an enormous **space vacuum cleaner**, clearing the **SOLAR SYSTEM** of **dangerous objects**.

In 2007 NASA's **New Horizons** *probe passed Jupiter on its way to Pluto, capturing images and taking measurements.*

Main antenna

Galileo's entry probe descended for 59 minutes to a depth of 125 miles (200 km) before disintegrating.

FIELD STUDIES

In 2000 the *Cassini* probe helped to map and visualize Jupiter's magnetic field and witnessed lightning at the poles, where there are continuous shimmering lights. Jupiter also has the most water in the Solar System—which contains particles from when the planet formed. In 2016 NASA's *Juno* probe should orbit very close to the surface to analyze these substances. But the radiation field is so strong, *Juno* will last only a year before breaking up.

Galileo's main antenna refused to deploy. So scientists reprogrammed the computers to use the small emergency antenna disc.

Juno (right) was launched in 2011. In 2016 it will overfly the polar region to uncover the mystery of the planet's magnetic "dynamo."

SATURN

Pale yellow Saturn is the farthest planet visible with the naked eye. This gas giant is celebrated for its amazing ring system, whose secrets are being revealed by the *Cassini/Huygens* mission.

Saturn's polar region has an unusual six-sided cloud system. The eye of the red-colored vortex is 20 times larger than Earth's biggest hurricane.

INSIDE SATURN

1. **UPPER ATMOSPHERE** Traces of ammonia and methane
2. **MAIN ATMOSPHERE** Hydrogen 97%, helium 3%
3. **CORE** Probably a thick metallic form of hydrogen, possibly with small rocky core about the size of Earth at its center
4. **PLANETARY RING SYSTEM** with Cassini Gap

Some **SCIENTISTS** think **SATURN** provides a **MODEL** of **how** our **SOLAR SYSTEM** formed some **4.6 BILLION YEARS** ago.

The Cassini probe is named after 17th century astronomer Giovanni Cassini. In 2004 it went into Saturn's orbit and released the Huygens lander to touch down on Titan. Cassini will end its mission with a controlled fall into Saturn's atmosphere in 2017.

MASSIVELY LIGHT

Although smaller than Jupiter, Saturn is still gigantic—760 Earths could fit inside. Internally it is similar to Jupiter, but with a cooler, less angry climate. Ammonia crystals in the upper atmosphere color the planet pale yellow. Average temperature is –288 °F (– 178 °C). Saturn's awesome rings are made of up of billions of pure ice fragments, probably the remnants of destroyed moons. More than 50 surviving Saturnian moons have been named.

Magnetometer boom

Radio/plasma wave subsystem antenna

Radioisotope thermoelectric generator (RTG)

Rocket engines

Huygens probe

Cooling fins

Antenna system

Like other deep-space craft, Cassini uses heat from radioactive decay to generate electricity.

GIRDLED BY MOONS

The moon Enceladus may contain salt oceans under its surface.

Titan, the largest of Saturn's moons, is big enough to hold an atmosphere. In 2005 *Huygens* successfully landed there (see page 24). The other moons vary greatly. Many, like Dione, are a mixture of rock and hard ice. Iapetus is clean on one side and spattered with soot from impacts on the other. Hyperion is shaped like a potato—possibly a comet captured by Saturn's gravity.

Some of the moons play a key role in shaping Saturn's fabulous rings. The orbit of Mimas pulls particles toward it, creating a gap called the Cassini Division. Other moons, like Prometheus and Pandora, orbit inside the rings and keep them in shape. *Cassini* is now on an extended mission to continue studies of the intricate Saturnian system.

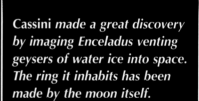

Cassini *made a great discovery by imaging Enceladus venting geysers of water ice into space. The ring it inhabits has been made by the moon itself.*

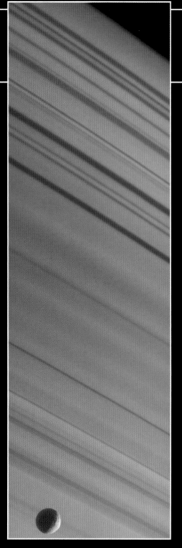

Viewed by **Cassini,** *Mimas shows against the majesty of Saturn's rings. This moon orbits well outside the rings. It has a huge crater from an ancient impact that nearly split it in half.*

Cassini's Saturn orbits have analyzed the density of ring particles. The icy pieces constantly collide with each other, shattering to make new surfaces that keep the rings shining brightly.

URANUS AND NEPTUNE

Puck

Due to an ancient collision with an Earth-sized planet, Uranus rotates with its axis at an angle of 82°. Circled by rings and moons, it resembles a celestial ferris wheel when viewed by the Hubble Space Telescope.

Juliet

● Miranda

Often called "ice giants," the two outermost planets are mysterious, frozen worlds. One is tipped crazily on its side, the other has ferocious, roaring winds.

Uranus' moon Miranda is a bizarre world of shattered and reformed ice canyons and ridges. One of these, Verona Rupes (indicated), is twice as high as Earth's Mount Everest.

Ariel ●

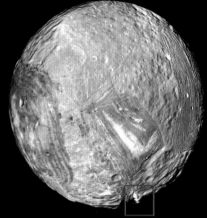

INSIDE URANUS AND NEPTUNE

1. **OUTER LAYERS** Hydrogen, helium, methane, with a thick hydrocarbon haze obscuring Uranus' clouds
2. **MANTLE** Water, ammonia, and methane ices
3. **CORE** Rock and ice

The **RINGS** of **URANUS** are the **DARKEST** objects in the **SOLAR SYSTEM**.

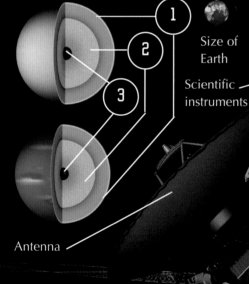

1

2

3

Size of Earth

Scientific instruments

Antenna

The two Voyager spacecraft are both the size of a small house. They were launched to take advantage of a rare alignment of the planets that happens once every 177 years. Each craft is powered by three radioisotope thermoelectric generators (RTGs).

Message from Earth

RTGs

TO THE ICE GIANTS

Uranus and Neptune are similar in size, and also similar internally to the other gas giants, except their mantles are made of chemical ices rather than metallic hydrogen. The only probe to visit was *Voyager 2* which left Earth in 1977, reaching Uranus in 1986. *Voyager* pictured the planet as a featureless pale greenish-blue globe. Coldest planet in the Solar System, Uranus can drop to −323 ºF (−192 ºC), but why it gives out so little heat is a mystery. Uranus also has 27 moons—cracked, cratered mini-worlds of rock and ice.

Uranus finally revealed some surface features in 2005 when the Sun passed over its equator and also highlighted its ring edges. One Uranus orbit lasts 84.3 Earth years.

The largest of Neptune's 14 moons, and the only one that is a sphere, Triton was visited close-up by Voyager 2. Thought to be a captured Kuiper Belt object (see page 28), it spins the opposite way to nearly every other planetary moon. Triton is slowly falling in orbit toward Neptune and ultimate destruction—in 3 billion years' time. The coldest body in the Solar System, it shoots out liquid nitrogen in geyser-like fountains.

STORM GIANT

Voyager 2 arrived near Neptune in 1989 to find a rich blue world (due to methane) with banded clouds and storm spots that race over the surface. In fact, Neptune has the highest sustained winds of any planet—up to 900 miles per hour (1,448 km/h). It has similar spin tilt to Earth, 28.3°, but its orbit takes 165 of our years and it receives only 1/1,000th of the sunlight here on Earth. With such wild weather, it is thought that rain on Neptune is in the form of methane crystal "diamonds."

A great dark spot, roughly the size of Earth, was seen by Voyager on Neptune. Neptune's spots are churning pressure storms that tear deep holes in the outer atmosphere, revealing the mantle below.

Neptune's faint and fragmentary ring system was imaged by Voyager 2.

VOYAGER 2 is now **leaving** the **SOLAR SYSTEM** to **probe INTERSTELLAR SPACE** until **2025** when its **power** will **DIE.**

PLANETARY MOONS

From bundles of space rubble to mysterious ice worlds that may harbor life, space exploration has revealed amazing variety in the 170-plus known planetary satellites of the Solar System.

Phobos, the largest of Mars' twin moons, orbits its parent planet closer than any other moon. In less than 50 million years, it will break up in the Martian atmosphere and become a planetary ring. Mars Reconnaissance Orbiter took close-up views of Phobos in 2007–08 revealing its dusty surface.

High-gain antenna

RADAR

PHOBOS

Spectrometer

Imaging camera

A FROZEN EARTH?

Mars' twin moons Phobos and Deimos may well be captured asteroids. Other moons are created when material hurtling in the orbit of a newborn planet clumps together and builds up until there is enough mass for the moon to become a sphere. This is probably what happened with Saturn's moon Titan—the only moon in the Solar System to have a thick atmosphere. In 2005 the *Huygens* probe landed on Titan as part of the *Cassini* mission (see page 20). As *Huygens* floated down on a parachute through the atmosphere, it saw a world that was alien—yet eerily familiar.

Huygens *operated in temperatures of −356 °F (−180 °C).*

Titan is the second largest moon in the Solar System.

Titan's upper atmosphere is 98.4% nitrogen, visible as a thin blue line (left). The only other nitrogen-rich atmosphere is Earth's. The moon's landscape is also strangely Earth-like (right). Scientists believe Titan resembles a primordial version of Earth, but deep-frozen, with a methane cycle instead of a water cycle.

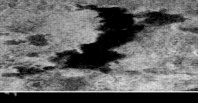

Titan's liquid methane raindrops fall like snowflakes in its low gravity and collect in lakes.

INSIDE EUROPA?

1. ICE SURFACE Cold (-200 ºF, -45 ºC) and brittle, seen to rotate independently of planet interior

2. SUBSURFACE WATER Liquid or slush convecting ice

3. MANTLE Rocky minerals

4. CORE Metallic elements

Galilean moons

Io   Europa   Ganymede   Callisto

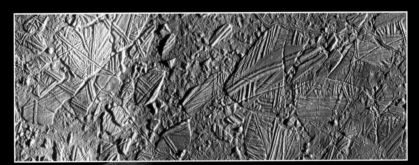

Io is a volcano world tortured inside by closeness to Jupiter's gravitational pull. Ganymede is the largest moon in the Solar System—bigger than planet Mercury. Of the four, only Callisto remains untouched by Jupiter's intense radiation.

WATERWORLD?

Could Europa's distinctive stained cracks be caused by types of primitive bacteria?

Jupiter's four largest or Galilean moons were first observed by astronomer Galileo in 1610. The second of these, icy Europa, has become a focus in the search for extraterrestrial life. Europa follows an elliptical (egg-shaped) orbit around Jupiter, causing tidal forces to stretch the moon. This heats and possibly melts its interior ice to make a subsurface saltwater ocean. Life flourishes on Earth in extreme cold with no sunlight—why not Europa? Europa could contain more water than all of Earth's oceans put together—*if* the clues on its surface hold true.

Europa's frozen surface (above) shows a cracked landscape similar to ice floes on Earth. The artist's impression below shows Jupiter as seen from the surface of Europa. ESA is planning to send a probe to Jupiter's icy moons in 2022.

EUROPA's flat **ICE SURFACE** **makes** it the **SMOOTHEST** **object** in the **SOLAR SYSTEM.**

ASTEROIDS AND COMETS

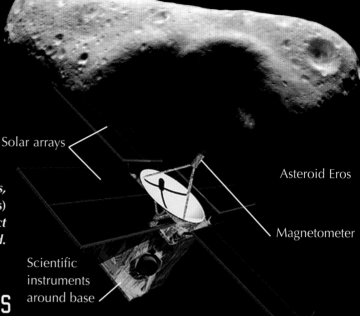

Asteroids are space rocks—leftovers from the Solar System's formation. Comets are icy bodies that are pulled in by the Sun's gravity from a distant realm way beyond Neptune.

The first asteroid orbited by spacecraft was 433 Eros, visited by NEAR (Near Earth Asteroid Rendezvous) Shoemaker in 2000. Eros was found to be a solid object about 4.5 billion years old.

Solar arrays

Asteroid Eros

Magnetometer

Scientific instruments around base

ROCK HUNTERS

Eros is about the size of the asteroid thought to have wiped out the dinosaurs on Earth 66 million years ago. Over 10,000 NEAs, Near Earth Asteroids, discovered so far have come from the Asteroid Belt, a thinly dispersed zone of debris between Mars and Jupiter. Asteroids range in size from dusty specks to the four largest—Hygiea, Pallas, Vesta, and dwarf planet Ceres. Together these form about half the mass of the Asteroid Belt. Scientists classify asteroids as carbon (C-type), silicate (S-type), or metal rich (M-type), depending on their content.

The Asteroid Belt probe Dawn visited Vesta (above) in 2011 and found a rocky body similar to a terrestrial world. Dawn will go on to orbit Ceres in 2015, which resembles an ice world. This should show why asteroids evolved so differently.

NEAR Shoemaker made a successful touchdown on Eros and found a thick layer of regolith—dirt and debris, similar to moondust.

> **ASTEROIDS** give us **clues** about **HOW** planets **FORMED** and **why** they **EVOLVED** in **certain ways**.

INSIDE CERES

1. **CRUST** Thin, dusty
2. **MANTLE** Water ice
3. **CORE** Rocky minerals

In 2010 Japan's Hayabusa probe returned samples from asteroid 25143 Itokawa to Earth. A more ambitious concept is to capture a whole Near Earth Asteroid and place it in orbit around the Moon. The NEA could then be mined for its valuable mineral content.

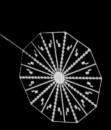

"Prior to Deep Impact we had almost no real knowledge of a comet's nucleus." Principal investigator Prof. Michael A'Hearn

As comets near the Sun, the solar wind vaporizes their solids to make a glow or coma around the head, and a long, fiery tail. Comets were long seen as signs of doom. In 1066 Halley's Comet appeared before England's fateful Battle of Hastings.

GIOTTO

*Halley passes Earth every 75 years and was studied up close by probe **Giotto** in 1986. Giotto found dusty black rock with less ice than expected.*

DEEP IMPACT

Sample return capsule

STARDUST

Impacter

High resolution imager

*In 2005 NASA's flyby probe **Deep Impact** released a small impacter to hit the surface of comet Tempel 3 (above). The cloud of ejected material was then analyzed revealing a surface like "talcum powder."*

*In 1999 NASA's **Stardust** probe flew into the coma of comet Wild 2 and collected a sample of dust which was returned to Earth in a capsule.*

A long-standing **THEORY says** that an ancient **COMET IMPACT** may have brought **LIFE** to **EARTH**.

COMET CHASERS

Comets are "icy rockballs," studied for their volatile (low boiling point) materials encased in loose build-ups of rock. They vary in size from 0.5 miles (0.8 km) to dozens of times larger. Their journeys around the Sun also vary greatly, from less than 200 years (short-period comets) to millennia (long-period comets). Most known comets came from the Kuiper Belt beyond Neptune (see page 29). Long-period comets travel from the very edge of the Solar System to be seen only once in recorded history. These mini-worlds offer a direct look at the Solar System's origins.

*In 2014 ESA's orbiter **Rosetta** will release a lander onto comet 67P/Churyumov-Gerasimenko to gather samples as it breaks up on its approach to the Sun.*

BEYOND THE PLANETS

In 2006 Pluto was demoted to dwarf planet status—a new category of world, massive enough to become spherical but lacking the gravity to make a clear orbital path.

NEW HORIZONS SYSTEMS

1. **RTG** Radioisotope Thermoelectric Generator
2. **REX** Radiometer measures atmosphere
3. **PEPSSI** Analyzes atmospheric ions (particles)
4. **SWAP** Solar wind and plasma recorder
5. **LORRI** Telescopic reconnaissance camera
6. **SDC** Counts amount of space dust on the probe

INSIDE PLUTO

1. **SURFACE** Nitrogen, methane ice, and frosts with seasonal melting
2. **MANTLE** Mixed rocks and ice
3. **CORE** Small, probably rocky

Pluto, seen from the Hubble Space Telescope, is a vague mass of light and dark.

DWARF WORLD

NASA's deep space probe *New Horizons* left Earth in 2004 to arrive at Pluto in 2015, with a closest approach of 7,800 miles (12,500 km). Scientists expect to see a rocky ice world with landscape features and a hazy nitrogen-based atmosphere. Pluto's orbit passes through the Kuiper Belt, a debris field of leftover material from the formation of the Solar System, where more dwarf planets have been discovered. Pluto has five known moons, the last discovered in 2012. It spins on its side, like Uranus, and rotates backward, like Venus, and does both slowly—one Plutonian day lasts 6.5 Earth days.

CHARON

High-gain antenna (hidden)

Radiation shield

Ultraviolet imaging spectrometer (hidden)

Visible/infrared imager/spectrometer

Pluto's largest moon, Charon, is one-eighth of its mass; Earth's Moon is one-eightieth of Earth's mass. Charon also orbits 20 times closer than our Moon orbits us. This makes Pluto and Charon tidally locked, spinning around as if tied by rope, always showing each other the same faces.

PLUTO is **15 times** more **MASSIVE** than **CERES**, our **nearest** dwarf **PLANET**.

Pluto's immense orbit is wildly elliptical. On its closest approach (perihelion) it is nearer the Sun than Neptune. As it moves farther away its atmosphere is thought to freeze onto the surface and so disappear.

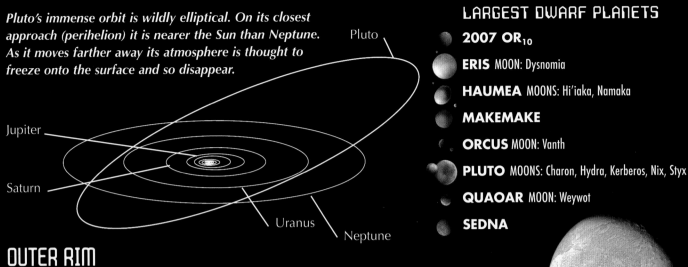

LARGEST DWARF PLANETS

2007 OR$_{10}$

ERIS MOON: Dysnomia

HAUMEA MOONS: Hi'iaka, Namaka

MAKEMAKE

ORCUS MOON: Vanth

PLUTO MOONS: Charon, Hydra, Kerberos, Nix, Styx

QUAOAR MOON: Weywot

SEDNA

OUTER RIM

After flying by Pluto, *New Horizons* will travel onward to the donut-shaped Kuiper Belt. This outer realm may contain thousands more dwarf planets—several have been discovered in recent years, although only the largest are named so far. Distant Sedna's orbit of over 11,000 Earth years takes it close to the farthest, coldest zone of the Solar System—the Oort Cloud. This has never been seen. But scientists use evidence from long period comets to theorize that the Oort Cloud may be like a much larger Kuiper Belt, but expanded as a vast spherical shell—truly the final frontier.

Eris is currently the largest dwarf planet. Its orbit takes 557 Earth years.

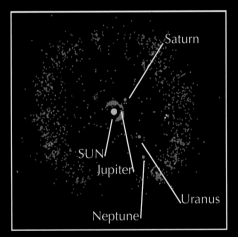

The Kuiper Belt is shaped like a donut or flattened disc. Comets from this region travel around the Sun on the same plane as the planets.

BEYOND the **KUIPER BELT** there **could** be as **many** as a **TRILLION** dwarf **planets** in the **OORT CLOUD**.

This artist's impression shows summer on Pluto. The surface frosts have evaporated and risen to form a haze. Pluto's weak gravity (one-sixth of Earth's) allows this thin atmosphere to spread far out into space.

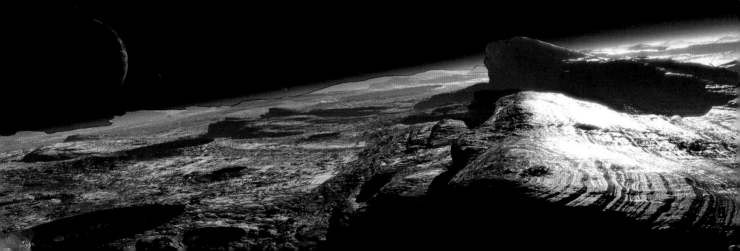

TECH FILES – SOLAR SYSTEM

SUN

DIAMETER 865,000 miles (1.39 million km)

MASS 333,000 times more massive than Earth

SURFACE TEMPERATURE 9,930 °F (5,500 °C)

ATMOSPHERE 73.5% hydrogen, 24.8% helium, oxygen, and other trace elements

MERCURY

DIAMETER 3,032 miles (4,879 km)

MASS 5.5% of Earth mass

TEMPERATURE 800 °F (427 °C) to -280 °F (-173 °C)

ATMOSPHERE Trace amounts of hydrogen and helium

LENGTH OF DAY 58.6 Earth days

LENGTH OF YEAR 87.9 Earth years

DISTANCE FROM THE SUN Min 28.5 million miles (48.9 million km), max 43.5 million miles (69.8 million km)

VENUS

DIAMETER 7,518 miles (12,100 km)

MASS 81% of Earth mass

TEMPERATURE Near constant 860 °F (460 °C)

ATMOSPHERE 96% carbon dioxide, 3% nitrogen, 0.1% water vapor

LENGTH OF DAY 243 Earth days

LENGTH OF YEAR 224.7 Earth days

DISTANCE FROM THE SUN Average 67 million miles (108 million km)

EARTH

DIAMETER 7,926 miles (12,756 km)

MASS Almost 6,000 billion billion tons

TEMPERATURE Average range 98 °F (37 °C) to -8 °F (-13 °C)

ATMOSPHERE 78% nitrogen, 21% oxygen, 1% argon

LENGTH OF DAY 23.93 hours

LENGTH OF YEAR 365 days

MOONS: 1

DISTANCE FROM THE SUN Average 92.9 million miles (149.5 million km)

MARS

DIAMETER 4,217 miles (6,787 km)

MASS 10% of Earth's mass

TEMPERATURE 98 °F (37 °C) to -190 F (-123 C)

ATMOSPHERE 96% carbon dioxide, 1.9% nitrogen, 1.9% argon

LENGTH OF DAY 24.4 Earth hours

LENGTH OF YEAR 686.9 Earth days

MOONS: 2

DISTANCE FROM THE SUN Average 141.6 million miles (227.9 million km)

JUPITER

DIAMETER 88,731 miles (142,800 km)

MASS 317 times more massive than Earth

TEMPERATURE Average at the cloud tops -243 °F (-153 °C)

ATMOSPHERE 90% hydrogen, 10% helium, 0.07% methane

LENGTH OF DAY 9.8 Earth hours

LENGTH OF YEAR 11.7 Earth years

MOONS: 65-plus, also faint rings

DISTANCE FROM THE SUN 483.6 million miles (778.4 million km)

SATURN

DIAMETER 74,974 miles (120,660 km)

MASS 95 times more massive than Earth

TEMPERATURE -301 °F (-185 °C) at equivalent of Earth's sea level pressure

ATMOSPHERE 97% hydrogen, 3% helium, 0.05% methane

LENGTH OF DAY 10.2 Earth hours

LENGTH OF YEAR 29.5 Earth years

MOONS: Over 60, also extensive ring system

DISTANCE FROM THE SUN 886.5 million miles (1426.7 million km)

URANUS

DIAMETER 31,763 miles (51,118 km)

MASS 14.5 times more massive than Earth

TEMPERATURE -323 °F (-192 °C)

ATMOSPHERE 83% hydrogen, 15% helium, 2% methane (at depth)

LENGTH OF DAY 17.9 Earth hours

LENGTH OF YEAR 84.3 Earth years

MOONS: 27, also dark ring system

DISTANCE FROM THE SUN 1.7 billion miles (2.8 billion km)

NEPTUNE

DIAMETER 30,775 miles (49,528 km)

MASS 17 times more massive than Earth

TEMPERATURE -373 °F (-225 °C)

ATMOSPHERE 74% hydrogen, 25% helium, 1% methane (at depth)

LENGTH OF DAY 19.1 Earth hours

LENGTH OF YEAR 164.8 Earth years

MOONS: 14 , also faint rings

DISTANCE FROM THE SUN 2.8 billion miles (4.4 billion km)

*Planets and Sun accurate for diameter scale but not distance

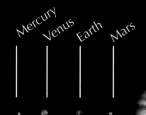

THE SUN

Mercury Venus Earth Mars

Jupiter

Saturn

Uranus

Neptune

GLOSSARY

ASTEROID relatively small, rocky, or metallic space object orbiting the Sun; most are between 33 feet (10 m) and 620 miles (1,000 km) across

ATMOSPHERE layer of gases around a space object such as a planet

COMET relatively small space object following a long, lop-sided orbit around the Sun, that warms and glows when near the Sun

CORE dense central region of a star, planet, moon, or similar space object

CORONA intensely hot region, usually of plasma, around space objects such as stars

CRUST hard outermost layer of a planet, moon, or similar space object

DWARF PLANET space object that orbits a star but has not cleared its orbit of other large objects

ELLIPTICAL oval-shaped, as for the orbits of many planets

FUSION in nuclear fusion, parts of atoms combine or join and give off energy, as when hydrogen atoms fuse into helium in the Sun

GRAVITY force of attraction between objects, which is especially huge for massive objects like planets and stars

MANTLE middle region, between the crust and core, of a planet, moon, or similar space object

MASS amount of matter in an object, in the form of numbers and kinds of atoms

MOON space object that orbits a planet

ORBIT regular path of one object around a larger one, determined by the speed, mass, and gravity of the objects

PLANET large space object that has a spherical shape due to its gravity, and has cleared a regular orbital path around a star

PLASMA one of four basic states of matter, similar to gas but the atoms or other particles have electrical charges, positive, or negative

PLATE TECTONICS system of large, rigid, curved, interlocking, slow-moving plates that form the surface of Earth and certain other planets

SATELLITE space object that goes around or orbits another, including man-made satellites and natural satellites like the Moon orbiting Earth

STAR space object that at some stage is large and dense enough, with enough gravity, to undergo fusion and give out light, heat, and similar energy

INDEX